Magellan's Shadow

Barbara Hemphill

Magellan's Shadow

Faith Poems

Barbara Booth Hemphill

Shadow Verse Press
Kingwood, Texas

Shadow Verse Press, Kingwood, Texas 77345

Printed in the United States of America

12 11 10 09 08 07 06 05 04   1 2 3 4 5

ISBN: 0-9761931-0-8

In memory of my aunt and uncle

Virginia and Walter Duhacsek

Having no children of their own
they gave birth to many dreams
through their generosity

Contents

Change

Healing

Light

Acknowledgments

Poetry and prayer are intensely personal expressions, so those who have enriched my life have enriched my writing as well. Many people have played a part in the creation of this book, as they accompanied me on the journey from which the writing emerged.

First, I am thankful to my husband Jim, who, besides being married to me all these years, assisted in making the cover design a reality. A man with many of his own creative talents, his encouragement of my writing has been constant and faithful.

My favorite poems in this collection are those that were inspired in some way by my son Chris. Being Chris' mother opened me to love in a way that profoundly influenced my poetry and my prayer. For all this and for much more than I can adequately express, I am grateful to him.

I also want to thank those who offered support, challenge, and encouragement as I explored these shadows — my dear friends Karen Rule, Liz Black, Alana Yuratich, Donna Martin, Patricia Taylor, and Marilyn Dill; and those who assisted me in their various professional capacities, especially Sr. Noel Toomey, Elise Gunst, Lee Ann Rathbun, Nancy Johnson, Bill Pemberton, and my colleagues in ministry at Good Shepherd Episcopal Church in Kingwood, Texas.

Finally, I need to thank those who helped me to think about God in new ways, particularly the faculty of Loyola Institute for Ministry in New Orleans, with special thanks to Michael Cowan and Regina Coll.

The Church says the earth is flat, but I know that it is
round, for I have seen the shadow on the moon, and I
have more faith in a shadow than in the Church.

Ferdinand Magellan

Magellan's Shadow

When priest and pope conspired to make earth flat,
Magellan must have laughed with heaven's moon,
who knew because she'd felt the shadow pass,
while he had seen on her the shape of truth.

Then speaking to Magellan, she proposed
a voyage that would test the power of faith —
a journey to the brink of the unknown,
then round its curve, her shadow his escape.

Sometimes when I look upon the moon,
the shadow that pursued Magellan's eyes
enchants my soul and fascinates my view.
She holds me in her curve of dark and light.

And there she speaks to me, and there invites,
and there she vows my voyages to lead.
If on her shadow I will stake my life,
then she will bend the world and curve the seas.

Now as a shadow settles on my soul,
I pray to know the courage of the moon —
constant in the darkness and the cold,
she waits, believing light is coming soon.

She pleads not for deliverance or escape;
she asks instead a blessing of the dark.
She wants to know its magnitude and shape;
she longs to feel its passage through her heart.

Magellan's shadow sent him round the earth,
"Impossible!" to those of straighter mind.
I see the moon again aflame with mirth
and wonder at the voyage she'll design.

Memory

The prophet Isaiah cried to the Lord and he brought the shadow back the ten intervals, by which the sun had declined on the dial of Ahaz.

2 Kings 20:11

The Man in the Moon

Sometimes when I sleep, you disappear.
I close my eyes for rest, and you
(thinking it a sleep of death?)
are stalked by fear.

You journey to the dark side of the moon.
When I awake and look around,
a silence pressing and profound
engulfs the room.

You stand amid the craters deep and wide,
the scars of ancient tragedies,
where orbiting antiquities
did once collide.

Vanished into darkness, you explore
the memories of cries and blows,
of nights that scarred your gentle soul,
that are no more.

A forming planet needs a circling moon
to shield it from the savage stones
the mighty universe has thrown,
that shout its doom.

And you, deprived of such a satellite,
with moon that fled or blew apart,
now bear the craters in your heart
into the light.

The Bulwark

A bulwark fallen into disrepair,
the evidence of battles lost in time,
when grief was given over to despair,
when feeling had not found its voice in rhyme.

Established to defend against the cruel assaults
of words that echo down the years,
behind it now, in still and silent pools,
lies grief, imbued with anger, become tears.

Though once it guarded well a holy place,
where only the high priest could enter in —
This symbol of protection, built by grace,
was then a sacrament of self-defense —

Inhabitants, enclosed in their lament,
who labored long to found a place of peace,
are now the prisoners of their best intents;
they long for their redemption and release.

Captivity has drained away their power
to openly resist those who encroach,
so fearfully, with strength only to cower,
they tremble at the gentlest approach.

The holy one now standing at the gates,
whose advent promises to bring relief,
awaits the invitation, hesitates,
then makes the preparation for a feast.

Wolf!

I remember when the wolf blew down my door —
cold fear, still tears,
hot breath, death threats,
and then it disappeared.
Everything I knew
flat on the floor.
I should have shouted, "Wolf!"
but who would hear?

"Never again," I swore, "Will *any* wolf
come here, breathe fear,
make me disappear!"
I built a house of bricks,
wise to his tricks,
a safer place than promises or arms.
I hid, unharmed.

And there I waited for a rainy day —
dark skies, moist eyes,
deep sighs, goodbyes,
a day to mark the end,
when I could spend what I had stored
that morning when the wolf blew down my door.

Interview with a Circus Lion

Simba, Simba, do you remember
before the shouts of popcorn vendors,
before the hoops, before the chair,
before the whip snapped in the air,
before you tasted sawdust fear,
before you slept in cages here?
Can you feel who you were then,
before the trespass of your den?
Who stilled the thunder of your roar?
Who sealed your spirit with these doors?
What robber snatched away your might?
What coward put your heart to flight?
Who now can venture with no doubt
to put his head inside your mouth,
knowing you will not bite down?
Your wildness has been turned around.
You've taken on yourself his fear;
He looks the part of courage here.
Without his whip, without his chair,
would he confront you anywhere?
Would you still jump from stand to stand
and leap through hoops to please the man?
And when he set the rings aflame,
would you ignite and take the blame?
Simba, take away his chair,
and jerk his whip out of the air!
Ignore the hoops, kick down the stands,
and test the courage of the man!
Let him know that you will bite,
if he insults your mouth tonight.
And as you watch him run away,
reclaim your strength of yesterday.

Demolition

Recalling his death, resurrection, and ascension,
we offer you these gifts.
The Book of Common Prayer

God, help me to recall his death
slowly, gently, breath by breath,
or with a gasp of sudden recognition,
as the framework of my vision
crumbles like an old downtown hotel
in the throes of demolition,
when gravity invites the walls'
descent into abyss.
A temporary cloud ascends, then falls,
unable to resist
the mystery of dust to dust.

God, grant me demolition's trust —
the hope of resurrection.

Anamnesis

*Do you still not perceive or understand? Are your hearts
hardened? Do you have eyes, and fail to see? Do you have
ears, and fail to hear? And do you not remember?*
Mark 8:17,18

O God, I don't remember,
and I've buried my desire
to retrieve the dreaded memories
from the ashes of the fire
that I kindled to consume them
when my heart became a liar,
when it spoke of fearful secrets
till my terror was inspired.

It confided scenes of horror
that my memory could not bear,
so I shoved it in the closet,
and I kept it hidden there.
I told it to be quiet;
I taught it not to dare.
So though the door is open now,
it doesn't seem to care.

It speaks no more of horror;
it shares no more its grief;
it dares not claim its freedom;
it shrinks into defeat.
It will not answer questions;
its truth now seems deceit.
Invited to communion,
it declines to take a seat.

O God, I don't remember,
and I don't know what to do.
I want to claim the memories
and to let them claim me too,
but my efforts seem so fruitless.
Still, my soul cries out to you.
For I know that you remember,
and your memories aren't consumed.

You were with me in the terror.
You were witness to the fire.
And your voice will not be silenced
by the death of my desire.
You were with me in the closet
where you kept the truth entire,
and you need not touch the embers
of my memory's funeral pyre

to retrieve the dreaded story
or to try to understand,
for my lifetime is recorded
in the creases of your hands.
And my terror is inscribed upon
your passion like a brand.
You can give me back my memories
and conclude what you began.

Reflections in the Lake

Empty-handed have I come among the dead,
no flowers for the stones and for the ducks no bread.
The prayers in my book have all been said.
Without a thought of consolation in my head,
I sit beside the lake and look with dread
upon the calm reflection of the life I shed —
When as a child I gave the ducks my bread,
I fed the lake my memories, crumbs of life instead,
to swallow all the fear my heart had kept,
to gobble up my anger ere the sun had set.
So now I seek to know what I forget,
to savor every tear that makes this lake so wet,
to gather to myself a child's regret,
to finally forgive the ones who owe this debt.
A cemetery lake may mirror yet
the story I first buried here among the dead.

Cocoon

When did I spin this small cocoon,
so snug, so dark, so safe,
so fit for only me?

When did I convince myself
that safety was enough
to get me through, enough
to last a lifetime?

When did pain become
my strongest enemy
and misplaced trust
my greatest fear?

How did I annihilate my need
for company, for care?
Where did I hide the longing,
or did I befriend it there?

What shadow made this darkness light
and helped me hope for wings?

My small cocoon,
Mystery-bearer,
Secret keeper,
Light in the darkness,
Hope of resurrection,
Faithful refuge,
The time has come for flight.

Hurricane in Key West

1.

I thought you were gone, blown over,
no longer a threat
to my world, my loves, my sense of things.
You hit the coastline long ago, far away,
and then you hesitated.
Knowing hesitation always leads to loss,
you took your time,
to maximize your casualties.
You found a needy place, a vulnerable town,
homes of branches and of tin,
dirt floors.
Boy, did you show them!
What courage you have, what power —
to overcome the poorest of the poor,
to decimate the innocent
with rain and twisting wind.
We were impressed.
We thought we'd seen the end.

Most hurricanes renounce their power
crossing over land,
as if the eye, seeing death for the first time,
winces in shame at what it has done
and repents of its destruction.
But you, with open eye,
declared the carnage good,
and finding yourself beyond the land,
you turned around to make another pass.
Your thirst still not assuaged,
you sought the open water
to regain your strength
and aimed directly for the Keys.

2

I thought you were gone, blown over,
no longer a threat
to my world, my loves, my sense of things.
But you've returned, heading straight for me,
no hesitation in your path,
ready to shatter me again.
You threaten me with howls.
You promise days of darkness and of thirst:
no power, no water, no phone.
You say I'll be alone,
or lying prone, a nameless casualty.
Boy, will you show me!
What courage you have, what power —
to make me bend or run away,
as I did then,
in fear of wind.
Well, I am not impressed,
for I have seen your end.

In passing over land, you lost your power.
Denial's strength cannot withstand
the eye's ability to see.
And though you howl familiarly, I know
that you are not the man you used to be.
You've kept your name, downgraded,
not a "hurricane."
Despite your bygone fame,
you're just a passing "storm."
Your run around the Gulf and through my life,
your legend of calamity,
ends here at lands' end.
I hold the Keys.

The Truth About Falling

Trauma leaves its clues —
evidence in language's effects,
wormholes leading to the past,
words that split my soul,
that place me in two worlds at once,
or else I am two *me*'s
in partial bilocation,
beaming up still incomplete.

World One — this realm of sense,
where voice and form appear,
home of *me* that stays in touch,
and looks back from the mirrors.

World Two – an insubstantial space,
where ghostly *me* resides,
hazy, nebulous, tiny droplets of myself
cling close, not quite together,
almost invisible, narrowly observant,
aware of them who aren't aware of *me*,
wishing they could see,
afraid they will.

A simple word
and misty *me* drops in
as if she fell with great acceleration
through the light-years gap that rends our worlds,
and landing, we are both surprised.
Cloven-hearted, double-minded,
forked tongued, and hyphenated,
I am beside myself.

The Plates

Long ago the land was one,
and at its edge was sea.
But underneath the unity
tectonic plates
began their slow dance round the world,
a covert dislocation,
and separated continents
that split the sea
became the only home humanity
would ever know.

Conceived in fractions
longing for the whole,
we do our best to live apart,
visiting the beach from time to time
to test the distance once again.

But underneath it all we feel
the shifting of the plates
and know
the fear of fragmentation.
The abyss of isolation
casts its universal spell.
Our wholeness, our connection
is recovered in an irony —
Our common human terror
is what holds us all together
as our continents drift further out to sea.

After a While

After a while
the quarter-inch tilt
the slight irregularity in walking
takes its toll.
And pain, shocking pain,
like lightning shoots from hip to heel.

It's then you know
the barely noticeable limp was real.

Not long ago
I thought it went away.
Adjustments here and there I'd made
to overcome a natural imbalance,
a childhood curvature.

As if to show
the scales by human means cannot be righted
and misaligned desire cannot be cured,
my overcompensation only cleared the way
for something even harder to endure –
this pain, shocking pain,
like lightning makes its startling appeal.

And now I know
the barely noticeable limp was real.

The Almighty

You who live in the shelter of the Most High, who abide in the shadow of the Almighty, will say to the Lord, "My refuge and my fortress; my God, in whom I trust."

Psalm 91:1-2

Blessed Are Those Who Mourn

"Blessed are those who mourn."
Then may my heart be torn asunder by your grace.
Let me know the wonder of your sorrow
in this time and in this place.

If those who mourn are blessed,
then let me be caressed by arms that know your grief,
And hold me through the storms that loose compassion
and the floods that bring relief.

Marshmallow God

Seeing the power of your fire,
watching the flames with blurring heat,
you look more like unquenched desire
than the God I see in church each week.

You are the fire of Pentecost,
not the neat row of teardrop flames
atop apostles' heads that pause
to have their image saved and framed.

There at the campouts of my youth
singing around the evening fire
you were the blaze of life and truth
we used to heat marshmallows on a wire.

How many marshmallows have I cooked
over a campfire well-contained?
Yours is the power I overlooked
hoping to sing away my pain.

You are an all-consuming fire;
you dance and dream and detonate.
Leaping the walls that cage desire,
you quicken, and you agitate.

I've had enough marshmallows in my time
to know that I long for something more —
The power of fire in a life divine
and a blaze that consumes my metaphors.

Angel of Grief

With bowing head and open wings,
burying your face in empty arms,
inclined against the hardness of the stone,
your posture yearning toward its strong support,
are you the God my heart is waiting for —
a God without a face that I can see,
with empty arms embracing poverty,
winged, but never flying from distress,
kneeling at the concrete hardened soul
to ask and offer only emptiness?

Has my rejection brought you to this grief?
Or have I touched your hem so often
that your strength is drained?
In all my searching I could not foresee
a God who hides her face,
mirroring my history of shame.
Unequipped to view your agony,
by this savage grace
my defense is slain.

What can I say to comfort you?
This dreadful stillness agitates my soul.
I cannot bear the silence, yet I dare not speak;
this moment's truth reveals mere words a fraud.

What can I do but kneel beside you,
covered by your wings?
I touch no more your hem
but reach across the cold, unyielding stone
to feel the emptiness within your arms,
to trickle with the tears along your cheek,
to share your grief and see the face of God.

A Covenant for the Imperfect

Pray in a way that fits your life.
Fall, then rise again.
Be weak, and trust in a power greater than yourself.
Accept necessary losses, to gain unnecessary graces.
Sin, and turn back when you see its evil.
Be angry, then forgive and reconcile.
Forgive freely, but not cheaply. (Take time to do it well.)
Accept the sickness required to become whole.
Make mistakes, admit them, then learn from them.
Cling to what you love; eventually let go.
Know your oppression, but seek release.
Make enemies, and love them.
Be rich, and be generous.
Mourn, and be comforted.
Hunger, thirst, and be satisfied.
Let your life become prayer.

The Emperor's Church
Has No Clothes

In memory of Lynda

I'm sorry …I just have to say this.
I … well … I just can't hold it in any longer.
God knows I've tried.
I keep asking, "Is it *me*? Is it *my* problem?
Am *I* seeing this the wrong way?"
I mean … Everyone else seems so happy.
They appear to be so satisfied
with all this superficiality.
At least, it seems superficial to me.
Maybe it's not to them – who knows?
But … well …This is my opinion,
and that's that.
I hope it doesn't offend you if I say this,
but if it does, then so be it.
I just can't keep silent any longer …

THIS IS SUCH A WASTE OF TIME!!
Don't you know what's valuable in this life?!!
We're talking about GOD here … GOD!!!
Creator of the universe!! Seen and unseen!!
Mystery, Ground of Being, Wellspring of Life!
Ah! So much love, so little time.
Please! Don't talk to me about teas
and silver services and bake sales.
There's so much more … so much more.
Talk to me about the much more,
about the much more of God.
Then we can really be together.
Talk to me … Talk to me.

The Bell of Mindfulness

Hear the ringing of the bell!
Come to peace … Attend … Be still.
Hear its echo in your heart,
how it calls your soul apart.
Let your being resonate with the bell's vibration.

Now your mind is letting go.
Soon your thoughts begin to flow
toward the One who calls you still
through the ringing of the bell
to the small simplicity of your meditation.

A Blessing, from Psalm 23

May goodness pursue you,
mercy renew you,
and love ripple through you
all the days of your life.

Small Things

a widow's mite
a lost coin
a little child
one talent
a mustard seed
leaven
five loaves and two fish
a baby in the womb
an iota of the law
bread and wine
a sparrow
two pennies
things that are not
things unseen
silence
a manger
in secret
the narrow gate
a cup of cold water
a seed
bread crumbs under the table

two or three together
the stone the builders rejected
two commandments
a touch
a cock crow
a speck in the eye
the finger of God
the hairs of your head
the unexpected hour
the very last penny
the lowest place
faith of a mustard seed
the eye of a needle
a denarius
a bush
a dream
a sigh
water
hunger
thirst
fragments of bread left over

Watch, therefore …

Nothing Matters

Notice the silence, the stillness, the void.
Enter the empty, invisible joy.
Seek out the quiet; abide in true rest.
Release acquisition; surrender conquest.

Search in the corners of life's small events
where blessings, like dust, gather as sacraments:
Signs of a presence unseen yet immense.
We sweep in the center and then we're content.

Our circumference is larger than commonly known,
the spaces called "empty", our veiled cornerstone.
This "nothing" believed is the fullness of life.
Discover that "nothing" in God will suffice.

Remembering Zacchaeus

Not too many things — and small —
linger on my way.
Gently, with a muffled call,
they wander through the day,

trying to observe me,
pushed backward by the crowd
of urgent incidentals
whose wheels are squeaking loud.

With holy perseverance
perhaps they'll climb a tree,
and over shouting circumstance
they'll perch where they can see.

Then, glancing upward, I'll perceive
the first that now are last.
These tiny ones will welcome me,
if only I will ask.

The One Who Receives, Asks

Answer me with asking.
Let me find a greater search.
When you open to my knocking,
may another door emerge.

Seasonal Haiku

Advent

Waiting for the One
Who came, comes, is coming soon.
Anticipation!

Christmas

God becomes human.
Angels sing, shepherds rejoice.
Let us adore him.

Epiphany

Bethlehem's bright star
directs the wise men's journey –
Light for all people.

Lent

Ashes to ashes –
Called into the wilderness,
we fast with Jesus.

Easter

Jesus is risen!
Even death is overcome!
What is this new life?

Ascension

Wait for the promise.
Jesus goes to the Father
to send the Spirit.

Pentecost

Flames, house-shaking wind
sending out disciples drunk
with Spirit, not wine.

Church of God the Homemaker

a dream

I met her for the first time in stained glass —
fingers buried deep within the dough,
wrists powdered with wheat flour,
earnestly kneading her prize,
transmitting with every squeeze and turn
her faith in bread's ability to rise.
The jar of leaven at her side
ensured the resurrection that, for now,
glimmered only in her eyes.
Kneeling at the rail below the glass,
"The body of Christ, the bread of heaven"
quietly disclosed
the gracious hospitality
of a home-cooked meal.
As I consumed, she pressed me to her loaf,
one more small ingredient in her healing recipe.

Our next encounter happened at the door.
Returning to my pew, I noticed it,
above the entryway, a hammered silver coin,
at least five feet across, slightly convex,
designed to carefully reflect
every single congregant,
each face in his or her own frame.
A large thumbnail, just visible along the lower rim,
powdered with the baker's same wheat flour,
evidence the coin was being held aloft with pride.
And underneath, the words,
"Rejoice with me!"
Awakening, I knew I had been found.

Change

Every generous act of giving, with every perfect gift, is
from above, coming down from the Father of lights, with
whom there is no variation or shadow due to change.

James 1:17

Waning

He must increase, but I must decrease.
John 3:30

Look! They're running out of wine.
What is that to you and me?
My hour has not yet come.

Their lamps will soon go dark
for want of oil.
Was it wise to leave behind
a sure supply?

And now the crescent moon
proclaims the dimming of the night.
Darkness grows,
the shadow glides,
until the faintest rim of light
is all remaining to our sight.

Soon and very soon
the now and the not yet
will collide, embrace,
collapse into each other —
blinded lovers intertwining in a swoon.
Then we will long for wine, for oil,
for lamplight, for the moon.

Night comes
when no one can work.

Hermeneutics and Heartsprings

Spiraling ever upward,
a heartspring within my soul
interprets my daily experience
and makes of the fragments a whole.
My words, my thoughts, my history,
the strands of a life entwined,
encompass a way of seeing
that rests in and reaches through time.
The world that existed before me,
the lives that preceded my birth,
are points on a widening spiral
that dwells in the heart of the earth.
And the spiral of my perception
extends from this circle of life;
I move with the thoughts of my mothers;
I dwell in the womb of their sight.

The world seems a vague repetition
of all that has happened before,
until by God's grace I encounter
a difference I cannot ignore.
A moment of stark revelation
or a quiet disturbance of mind
breaks into my heartspring's contentment
to reveal a deception that blinds.
The points on my spiral then cower
and ask for permission to stay,
for some in this moment gain power,
but others must be thrown away.
The spiral now changes position,
reorders the points that remain,
and enters again the encounter,
interpreting unknown terrain.

Interpreting letter by spirit,
the spring in my soul unwinds
as it senses the text's own heartspring
and follows after its kind.

The heartsprings from two horizons
first touch in a glancing blow
then meet and begin discussions
and tangle the further they go.
At some points they stick together;
at others they stay far apart.
Sometimes there's a painful twisting
as a tangled wire catches my heart.

Jarred by the pain, awakened,
my eyes open wider to see
an alternate view before me,
a transformed reality.
Patterns I never noticed
appear in the same old lines,
and life as it stands before me
confronts me with new designs.
The heartsprings release their tension,
empowering action for change.
Not only is thinking reordered;
my whole life must be rearranged.

Such is the power of heartsprings,
of spirals interpreting text,
of classes that teach hermeneutics,
of moments that sting and perplex.

For My Son

This is my Son, the Beloved, with whom I am well pleased.
Matthew 3:17

A single cell, incarnation
of two histories in human shape,
develops and grows,
tests his boundaries with blows,
begins yearning for his escape.

He has outgrown his home near his mother's heart,
and he hears his own rhythm outside,
so mother and son
move in labor as one,
for this passage cannot be denied.

Even now as you press through the darkness of life
into dwellings of broader scope,
my womb can't relax
as my heart contracts
to deliver a fragile hope.

We are joined once again in the travail of birth,
and although not a word is spoken,
I perceive that my pain
echoes your soul's refrain,
for the cord has been cut, but not broken.

As I grieve in your labor of passage today,
I'll rejoice in the life that proceeds,
for you are my son,
my beloved, the one
with whom I am well pleased.

Tourist

I'd know it anywhere,
the gait, the tousled hair,
the posture of young confidence
approaching on this road
half a world away from my belonging.

When we greet I reach up,
rising on tiptoe to kiss your cheek,
while you bend down to me.
It used to be the other way around.

Now I rely on you to teach
the words and customs of this place.
Who will hold my trust
and keep my journey safe?
You bear the wisdom here
and I the need of grace.

Pointing out the window of the bus,
"What's that?" –
your question twenty years ago.
Now patience, names, and histories
reverse their flow,
honoring my asking and my eagerness to know.

How quickly life inverts
our size, our reaching, and our roles!
Once I was your home,
and "Fly Me to the Moon" your mobile's song.
Now you have flown,
and I am just a tourist
in this world where you belong.

Birth to Bronxville

When you were born
they laid you in my arms.
You slept, caressed,
nourished at my breast.

There was so much to know, to see.

I knew
> that you would look like me
>> or speak like me
>> or write or walk
>> or laugh like me
> — and yet like you.

I knew
> that you would talk
> that syllables would gather into words
>> and words would wander into sentences
>> and paragraphs and stories
> and you would tell me of your dreams.

I knew
> that you would walk
> that your steps would make a path
>> and paths would trace a journey
> and some day
>> you would journey far
>> away from me.

I knew so many things
I was prepared
except for this,
that no one shared.

I never knew
    that as you grew
    my heart would fall in love with you;
    a different kind of love, it's true,
        but just as great a fall.

I never knew
    your voice, your touch
    could leave this silence,
    offer such an emptiness,
    a hollow hush
        that settles in the hall.

I never knew
    that when you left
    my arms, my heart, my hands, my breast
    would grieve with aching loneliness,
        as if you were my all.

When you were gone
I laid you in my heart
most tenderly,
so I could set you free.

There was so much to know, to see.

Evidence of Absence

My heart can touch the distance
as it reaches toward your face.
My arms embrace the emptiness
that stands here in your place —
the evidence of absence,
missing life in hollow space.
I listen to the silence,
laughter's echo long erased.
I cling to priceless vacancy
whose outline I can trace.
You moved beyond my arms' reach,
but you've molded my embrace
so that even in your absence
I conform to fit your shape.

The Mother of the Bridegroom

As she walks the aisle of promise,
faithful to fulfill her part,
simple prayers of reminiscence
flood the chambers of her heart.
Anchored safely in the darkness
move the remnants of her dreams —
moments past, with love remembered.
Every step recalls a scene
of his boyhood effervescence,
of his laughter ringing clear;
flash and glimmer of remembrance
reach through her across the years.
Here a treasure of caresses;
here so many sad goodbyes;
first the welcome, then the parting,
each a glimpse of paradise.

For the sake of celebration,
for the honor of his bride,
by the power of her memory
she will tuck her tears inside,
greeting every glad companion
with a smile of fond embrace.
Only skillful intuition
could find sorrow in her face.

Till his wedding day is over,
and her guests have wandered home,
when the mother of the bridegroom
will be left to dance alone
in her darkness drawn from memory,
in her silence bathed in light,
in her stillness filled with music
that reminds her of his life.

Untimely Death

Balanced at the brink of life's arrest,
where comprehension vanishes to faith,
my search for holy meaning in this death
stands paralyzed, enveloped in heartache.

Darkness seems to weigh upon my breath
as if the air were filled with heaven's grief.
Silence bears the song of God's distress,
agony no human voice can speak.

Nuisance

There you stand
rooted and unmoved
by my beloved plans
to build a patio and pool
upon this land.

You with your cones,
your needles poised to fall
onto the walkway stones;
You'll mar it all
if left alone.

We have other trees
that don't require as much as you.
They drop their leaves
but wait until the weather cools.
They live to please.

But you — you just will not desist!
You drop your needles in the pool
and deem your cones a gift.
You must think me a fool,
or else a pantheist.

You shall be gone,
you with your peculiar ways.
The lines are drawn,
and I will spend my days
in landscaped calm.

Regency, 100% Cotton

Draped across the chair
tattered edges, faded green,
your name tag curling up
from years of washings
proclaims your high ambitions,
your fabled purity,
grand potential trapped within
the cotton loops of terrycloth,
or hiding in the seams that, torn,
now finger out like tentacles
to gather younger garments,
to strangle now and then,
as if their aspirations,
their straight, bright tags,
bearing your name,
evoke too many painful memories.

You, who now endure the cars,
the windshields, floors,
who man the front where pesticides and wax
assault your fray,
were once the elegant décor,
an ornament selected for your comeliness,
your loveliness of form.
For this you ache,
believing you've betrayed your lofty dreams.

Do not seize the young, or strangle them,
but let them turn and toss and agitate
and find their way to fray into redemption.
The cars can wait.

The Adventurer

The word of God seemed eager to avoid her;
no hound of heaven loosed to bring her back.
The region she had left to reconnoiter
named "mystery" in every almanac.

With "terra incognita", "here be dragons,"
warnings shouted from the pages of her book.
But she set off nonetheless to do her tracking,
and she never gave her life a second look.

September Sky

Remembering September 11, 2001

A childhood near the airport
drew my vision toward the sky.
God's heavenly home was brimming
with tourists, I was sure,
waving from their windows to everyone below.

I loved the observation deck
in the days when it was safe
to stand atop the concourse
and wave and watch and wave,
a nickel for a closer look through huge binoculars.

The engines' drone,
the sight of dropping wheels,
the glint of steel,
the over-passing wings,
are means of grace for me.

September's tragedy
hijacked my cherished altar,
defiled my sanctuary,
turned celestial sacraments to choking dust.

History's first, they say,
since people moved by plane –
those grounded flights,
that empty, silent sky.
Even clouds seemed hesitant that day.

The sky was changed forever
desecrated by the terror
it paused, shamefaced and mute,
its violation clear.
Now every plane reminds me of the final calls,
men choosing how to die.

I look up to the heavens and remember
people waving from their windows
to everyone below.
I wave
and pray the tourists home.

Healing

… so that they even carried out the sick into the streets, and laid them on cots and mats, in order that Peter's shadow might fall on some of them as he came by.

Acts 5:15

Side by Side

To venture all alone into the canyons of the soul,
to wander where the riverbed is dry,
to climb in isolation to the peak of transformation,
a migration up the inner mountainside,
exhausts the soul's resources,
saps her power,
steals her nerve,
encourages the valiant heart to hide.
Courageous exploration yearns for gentle consolation;
the journey needs companions and a guide.

Though we seek our destination
with a sense of desolation,
consecration to the God of all goodbyes,
let's remember that we travel side by side.

Giver of Grace

Giver of grace,
love of my soul,
home where my faith rests,
my life's highest goal:
By your grace make me whole.

Creator of life,
sustainer of peace,
in your presence all strife,
all dissension, must cease:
May your presence increase

till each thought, word, and dream
in my heart is your will,
till my every desire
is a wish you've instilled,
and your dream is fulfilled.

God's Dismay

... you had established me as a strong mountain; you hid your face;
I was dismayed.
Psalm 30:7

O gracious God, be not dismayed!
I have not turned from loving you.
I did not know, I could not see
beyond the form I'd given you.

The thought of your embracing love,
your wounds, your terror, and your tears,
was greater than my heart could bear,
and so I looked away in fear.

I built a prism to refract
the light I could not long behold.
Then, gazing on the scattered rays,
I misconstrued a calf of gold —

an image of a lesser god,
abstracted from the greater whole,
a god omnipotent and wise,
the creature of a changeless mold.

When this god failed, for want of heart,
in dark distress I hid my face,
but searching in the emptiness
you found me, and I found your grace.

Face to Face

Oh, to see beyond the boundaries of my vision,
to hear the music of that silent land,
to feel the movements of divine compassion,
to know the love I cannot understand!

I long to burst the bonds of my condition.
I search to find a pathway to your door,
for everywhere I stand in incompleteness,
and always you invite me to your more.

The yearning of my heart defies expression.
Its silence sings the rhythm of your grace,
and dancing to a melody of questions,
my soul at last beholds you face to face.

A Prayer for Listeners

Gracious God, you formed our hearts.
You know our going out and our coming in.
You stand at the doorway of our souls
and at the boundaries of our lives,
always inviting us
to go out beyond the limits of our experience,
to come more deeply within ourselves.

As we journey with you —
going out and coming in,
may we find your ways in the unknown,
        see your face in the unexpected,
        meet your grace in the unfamiliar.

As we listen for the breath of your Spirit,
may we hear deeply, reverently, tenderly enough
        to feel what you feel,
        hurt where you hurt,
        desire what you desire,
so that your gracious power
may be manifest in our midst.

A Hysterectomy Prayer

Holy Mother,
in you we live and move and have our being.
With compassion you caress us,
nourish us,
enclose us,
protect us,
as we grow into the fullness of our humanity.

You accompany us in labor
as we are born
again and again
to new life in you.

Like you,
my womb has nourished and embraced new life.
It knows the labor and pain of birth,
of loving and letting go.
It has taught me much about you,
and about myself.

But now, for the sake of my own well-being,
I have to go on without it,
and saying goodbye is never easy for me.

Mother-God, be with me in this labor.
Enclose me in your womb,
even as I surrender mine.
Nourish me with your compassion.
Make me womb-like
in my womb-lessness.

A Prayer When a Child Has Died

Tender God, you hold our children in your arms
and keep them in your powerful embrace.
This we know by faith.
But now this child has died
and the mystery is greater
than we have strength to face.
Uphold us by your grace,
surround us with your love,
until we trust again
in your goodness,
in your gentle, kind attraction.
Let our grief become a source of simple strength
and our tears a fountain of compassion.

Dispossess Me of Myself

God of the Beatitudes, dispossess me of myself.

I offer you what I know and own and am,
what I think and believe and love,
all that fills and satisfies and delights me.
Give me ignorance and absence
that incarnates your wisdom.
Grant me darkness and emptiness
that contains your light.
Give me stillness and silence
that dances to your music.

Take my hope, my meaning, my desire.
Let me despair of them and mourn their loss
until I find, in that despair and in that mourning,
the darkness of your hope,
your meaning,
your desire for me.

May I yet arrive where I am not,
possessing what I do not own,
understanding what I do not know,
believing what I doubt,
loving what I care nothing about.

God of the Beatitudes, dispossess me of myself.

Myrrh Bearers

When death is put away,
hastily entombed and closely guarded
lest the stone be rolled aside
and grief escape
into the hearts of true believers,
then we appear — myrrh bearers
come to anoint the dead,
to reach into the grave
with sense and smell,
the aromatic oils in our possession
fragrant reminders
that what in haste was buried
remains a treasured part of life.

Sometimes our desire
to honor the discarded halts
with angel voices,
empty shrouds,
absent stones
proclaiming unexpected resurrection.
Then we return — myrrh bearers
come to anoint our friends
with aromatic life.

A Prayer For Those Who Cannot Do the Hokey Pokey

O God who spins the earth and tilts its axis,
bless those whose leaning keeps them from the dance
and those who suffer dizziness when turning all about
and those without their legs or feet or hands.

I pray for those so far outside the circle
they cannot even think of stepping in,
for those who stand surrounded by a barrier of fear
and dare not place a foot beyond the rim.

O God who starts the universe to dancing,
who sets us in the curves of space and time,
bless those whose pain in bending forces them
            to stand erect
and those who have a surgeon-straightened spine.

Bless those who tremble constantly with palsy
and those so scared or weak they cannot shake
and those too deaf to hear the song's instructions
            to the crowd
and those who will not dance for heaven's sake.

O God who keeps the galaxies in orbit,
who makes the sun traverse from east to west,
bless those who cannot do the hokey pokey just because
they do not know their right side from their left.

One Stone at a Time

I said, "I have a bulwark deep inside."
"We could take it down together,
one stone at a time"
was her reply.
Her answer was alive.

It flowed, then settled over me,
a fluid trust that soaked my sense of doom.
The hope that hid so long behind the rocks
began again to hum its tune,
though quietly.

The regular connection over years,
a gathering of stories, laughter, tears,
and underneath them all her love and care,
concern for things I couldn't even see,
concern for me,

became the substance of a confidence
that built another structure in my soul,
of metaphor and song and sacrament,
more stable yet more fluent than the last,
to aid collapse.

So empathy's compassion overcame.
Concrete, mortar, bricks and stone
eventually gave way,
and lurking shadows breathed again
the air of faith.

Stones We Leave Behind

This gathering of stones,
memento of holy encounter,
ineffable infusion
remembered without words.

A new name given
in syllables of spirit,
A covenant
in articles of faith,
A heart transformed
by shadow of turning.

Here that heart was emptied.
At this place it expelled them,
flung them at the enemy
for the last time.

So they fell
into this calm array,
forever signing the site
a portal to eternity —
Beth-lehem,
house of daily bread,
where water becomes wine
and flows from living springs
when stones give way to flesh.

Angels of Gethsemane

Remembering September 11, 2001

When memory brims our hearts with terror
and our eyes with tears,
remain with us,
watch and pray,
"Remove this cup, O God, ..."
Our faith is fear.
May angels of Gethsemane
surround us here.

Song and Response

Lee Ann's Song

I wanted to grieve with you, but you wouldn't let me.
As fast as my heart pursued, you hurried away.
Fearing compassion's touch, you fled from my kindness,
disguising your pain in such beguiling array
that only the speckless eye could witness your anguish,
could know you were terrified, alone and afraid.
I offered to comfort you, to sit in your darkness.
My tenderness you refused; you thought yourself brave.

Alone with your wounded heart, you've finally faltered.
Your fortitude blown apart by the terrible weight
of bitterness unexpressed and long-contained sorrow.
Your ancient and deep distress throws off its restraint
to look for a surer home, a trustworthy shelter.
It flees toward the catacombs, a holy escape.
Before you again are lost in darkness and silence,
consider and count the cost of hiding this way.

No refuge can understand your unspoken questions.
No fortress can take your hand and fill you with grace.
No darkness can overcome the light in your suffering.
No silence can make you dumb; it voices your rage.
My heart is a safe retreat, a quiet enclosure
that welcomes your deepest grief and offers embrace.
I still long to share with you the depth of your sorrow.
I wept when your heart withdrew; I miss you today.

My Response

Little did you know
that when you spoke that day
you spoke for God,
inviting me into my depths,
my endlessly avoided void
beneath forgotten threats.

Little did you see
that when I looked away
your tender glance
pursued and haunted my retreat
until my vision was all eyes
and gaze with gaze could meet.

Little did you feel
that when I recognized
what I had missed
resistance yielded to regret
that birthed a sacred shadowing
whose gifts awaken yet.

Sign of the Cross Healing Prayer

From the top of your head
to the soles of your feet
and from one side to the other
may the Almighty heal you.

In your memories of the past
in your hopes for the future
and in this present moment
may the Almighty heal you.

In your mind
in your heart
in your soul and in your strength
may the Almighty heal you.

Light

… the people who sat in darkness have seen a great light, and for those who sat in the region and shadow of death light has dawned.

Matthew 4:16

The Shaded Moon

We are children of the light,
radiance-born,
propelled by resurrection.

I saw the moon eclipsed tonight;
its shaded form
no luminous reflection

became an ember divinized,
with scars adorned,
ablaze in imperfection.

St. Valentine's Day 2002

A card on the microwave isn't too sweet,
but Lent came early this year,
making candy, which he always gives up,
a tasteless Valentine.

So love seeks sugarless expression
in the words of a greeting card
sealed with sour glue
attached with invisible tape
to the transparent glass
of an instant oven.

It is love nonetheless,
enduring through bitterness,
secretly fastening,
soul-revealing,
instant yet everlasting.

Invisible Embrace

Ah, God!
Transparent, sacred breath,
concealing love in blind caress,
not heard, or felt,
or touched, or spoken,
that brands the soul
and leaves her broken
open to your next embrace.
Longing and unveiled
she waits.

I Would Dance with Teresa

What is this heavenly music,
its rhythm awakening my soul?
And where will this melody take me
if I yield to its ebb and its flow?

It calls me to leave on a journey,
a pilgrimage much like a dream,
to visit the sacred memorials,
to photograph landmarks unseen.

This is a journey of spirit,
a wandering, aimless retreat
directed by heavenly strangers
whose wisdom defies my belief.

They lead me with harmonies higher
than any of thought or of word,
to overcome logic's resistance
and take me into the absurd.

Theirs is the land of the music.
Theirs is the rhythm of life.
Theirs is the dance of the ages.
Theirs is the song of delight.

But where is the heavenly partner
who leads me to move with their dance,
who trains me to sense higher rhythms,
who teaches the notes of their chants?

How can I learn without teaching?
How can I go, if not led?
How can I sing without music?
How can I dance when I'm deaf?

Send me a traveling companion
who moves with the rhythm of life,
for I would dance with Teresa
to heavenly music tonight.

You Delight in Me

You delight in me.
Gathering your dreams in love's desire,
you put my soul to flight in me
with dancing fire.

Evening Star

Why do you hide behind these clouds,
Radiance obscured?
The entire sky, turning its gaze,
witnesses your fire.

Brilliant summons to night's new birth,
you lure, then vanish,
playing hide and seek at sunset,
my heavenly child.

I cannot forget your brightness,
Promise from the past.
Like the wise men, Bethlehem's kings,
I journey starward,

blind to both my destination
and my history,
for you, O Evening Star, possess
my hope's beginning.

Screen Saver

We have a new screen saver,
a photograph I took when we were there.
Stepping through an ancient archway
into St. John's College square,
as you approached the central green
you stopped and stared
as if to measure history
or contemplate a destiny
that hovered in the atmosphere.

I aimed my lens at you,
or at your dream,
and now that stillness,
that long breath of English air,
that gaze is saved
on our computer screen.

I sit amazed and wonder what you see.
What captivating vision holds you fast?
It must be something beautiful and vast,
and lovely as your looking looks to me.

Wisdom

Wisdom seeps through cracks
wherever microscopic gaps allow her
minimal freedom, autonomy of space.
Resistance cannot quench her longing
in a universe of such vast emptiness,
her home, unnoticed in the busyness of time.

Wisdom waits in silence,
and hopes, for visitors,
guests awakened to her prefix of desire –
brief beginnings, bare parting of lips,
doorways to her world.

"Un-", she says, or "de-",
extending her gracious invitation,
and suddenly the wise become undone —
inspecting the unseen,
weighing the unknown,
craving decrease and detachment.

Wisdom's children seep through cracks
wherever microscopic gaps allow them
minimal freedom, autonomy of space.
Resistance cannot quench their longing
in a universe of such vast emptiness,
their home, unnoticed in the busyness of time.

The world was created through Wisdom,
yet the world does not know her.
Daily she visits her people,
and her own people do not receive her.
But to all who receive her she gives power
to become children of God.

Light the Torch of Your Salvation

When your people, slaves in Egypt,
cry to you in their distress,
Moses hears your voice ablazing,
"Bring them to the wilderness."

> *Chorus: Give me hope to comfort your people;*
> *Give me strength to bear your word;*
> *Light the torch of your salvation*
> *Holy, holy, holy Lord.*

When the world is lost in darkness,
when the time for grace has come,
Light becomes a human baby,
"You will bear my holy son."   *Chorus*

Dove descending from the heavens,
Jordan's Spirit-sign to John,
holy thunder shouts rejoicing,
"This is my beloved son."   *Chorus*

Flames of Spirit rest upon us
giving us the power of God;
Jesus fills us with his passion,
"Take and eat my Body and Blood."   *Chorus*

Give us hope to comfort your people;
Give us strength to bear your word;
Light the torch of your salvation
Holy, holy, holy Lord.

Black Hole Song

Devouring darkness, Perseus' black hole,
Son of Zeus, the God of gods,
your universe-inhaling heart
absorbs adjacent galaxies
consuming stars
till light itself becomes your sustenance.

Unseen, so undeterred,
you recall time, space, sound.
"Speak of this to no one."
"Let the deed proclaim itself."
Sole evidence a humble melody,
an X-ray tune too deep for human ears,
a low B flat that resonates throughout the universe,
ten million years' expanse between the waves.

You manifest your loveliness most gloriously in silence;
extinguishing our ordinary light,
your radiance invisibly suffuses constellations.
The cosmos knows its temporary plight
is held within a darkness that composed the lullaby
intoned since galaxies were given life.

The Thank You Note

She had much to be thankful for,
my grandmother would say.
It seemed to me she often built her own blessings.
She was decent and good, honest and diligent,
and she loved to laugh, especially with friends.
She married a man of similar integrity,
who played his own small part in saving Europe,
a Rainbow Division M.P.

A thank you note was all she ever asked,
within the courteous time frame, of course,
and written by hand.
Her notes usually arrived the day after the gift,
an amazing feat —
unless she missed the house number or zip,
which happened more frequently in her later years.

When the call came I was at a coffee shop.
She was confused, they said,
agitated, restless to the point of violence.
The ambulance was on its way.
I met her in the ER,
where, for almost the last time,
she put my name and face together
in a single memory.
In just a week she crumbled into death.
Bones gave way to agonizing pain,
vision turned dark,
the world that had so blessed her
became a frightening enemy.

Morphine arrived just later than the need,
and could not win its race with suffering.
She cried for help, not knowing what she meant.
I cried beside her, understanding more.

I stood by through it all,
inadequate answer to her hopeless cry.
I don't know how I stayed.
I don't know why I never disappeared, or hid inside;
I sorely sought the gift.
And then she died.

Within the courteous time frame of her death,
and by my own left hand,
I wrote this thank you note ...

Dear Aunt Virginia,

*Thank you for time under your trees, for the sound of cattle beyond
your fences, for the fragrance of your perfume and of fresh manure
in Uncle Walter's garden, for evenings watching home movies of
Christmases and your exotic vacations, for the music of your
laughter, your stubborn optimism, your exuberant self-assurance,
and your quiet generosity. It was an awful week for both of us, but
its pain can not erase my half-century of gratitude. I hope this note
arrives in a timely fashion, as I am unsure of the zip.*

Love,
Barbara (your favorite niece)

God Waits in Silence

God waits in silence

Eventually all things return
to the good
to God

for words can only go so far
ideas have their limits
images fade in darkness

In time they reach their end
in silence
in emptiness
in longing
in God

who waits
open-armed
for their return.

Eclipsed

We are children of the light,
pure radiance streaming.
I saw the moon eclipsed tonight,
our shadow gleaming.

Notes

"Magellan's Shadow"; epigraph is attributed to Ferdinand Magellan, the Portuguese navigator, in *The Great Quotations* (George Seldes, ed., 1967, Pocket Books, New York). Seldes' reference for the quote is Ira Cardiff, *What Great Men Think of Religion*.

"Demolition"; epigraph is from the Episcopal *Book of Common Prayer*, page 363, Eucharistic prayer A in the Holy Eucharist Rite II liturgy.

"Anamnesis" is the Greek word for *remembrance*, used in Luke 22:19, "Do this in remembrance of me."

"Hurricane in Key West"; In 1998 Hurricane Mitch blew westward through the Gulf of Mexico, crossed over Central America into the Pacific, and returned to the Gulf for another pass. We were vacationing in Key West when it arrived there.

"Blessed Are Those Who Mourn" is a response to Matthew 5:4.

"Marshmallow God"; My aunt lived on 60 acres in Sugar Land, Texas — now Duhacsek Park. After my uncle died, we helped her with clearing and burning brush. After I kept watch over a fire my husband had started, I wrote this poem.

"Angel of Grief" is a response to a photo of the monument William Wetmore Story sculpted in 1895, for his wife Emelyn's grave.

"The Emperor's Church Has No Clothes" was written in memory of my friend Lynda Reisenleiter. I wrote it in her voice; I read it at her funeral.

"Remembering Zacchaeus" refers to the story in Luke 19:1-10.

"The One Who Receives, Asks" responds to Matthew 7:7,8.

"Seasonal Haiku"; seasons of the church year.

"Church of God the Homemaker" alludes to Luke 15:8-10 and Matthew 13:33.

"Waning" alludes to John 2:1-4, Matthew 25:1-13, John 9:4.

"Hermeneutics and Heartsprings" was written for a class taught by Dr. Michael Cowan at Loyola University, New Orleans – Loyola Institute for Ministry. Hermeneutics is the study of principles of textual interpretation. The process can be visualized as a spiral.

"Tourist"; My son Chris spent one undergraduate year at Wadham College, Oxford University. We visited him in March 2000.

"Birth to Bronxville"; Chris completed his undergraduate work at Sarah Lawrence College in Bronxville, NY.

"Nuisance" was inspired by the story of a woman who was planning to install a swimming pool in her back yard. She first had to remove nearby pine trees.

"September Sky" is a remembrance of the days immediately following September 11, 2001, when all planes were grounded. It is a response to Isaiah 51:6, and to images of people trapped in the Twin Towers, waving for help to those below on the streets.

"Dispossess Me of Myself" is a response to "East Coker" (III) by T. S. Eliot.

"Myrrh Bearers" alludes to the icon of the same name (also called "The Holy Women at the Tomb"), based on the resurrection story in Mark 16:1-8.

"A Prayer for Those Who Cannot Do the Hokey Pokey" is a response to the question, "What if the Hokey Pokey really is what it's all about?" which I first encountered on a Cards by Anne greeting card, www.cardsbyanne.com.

"Song and Response"; My supervisor in Clinical Pastoral Education spoke the first line of *Lee Ann's Song* in an evaluation session. The words affected me in a powerful way, framing my spiritual journey for several years afterward. *My Refrain* attempts to express her *Song*'s effect on me.

"Sign of the Cross Healing Prayer" is designed to be prayed while making the sign of the cross three times over the person for whom the prayer is offered.

"I Would Dance with Teresa" refers to Teresa of Avila, the great Spanish mystic, spiritual writer, and teacher of prayer (1515-1582).

"Evening Star" is a response to the Georgia O'Keeffe watercolor painting by the same name, painted in 1916.

"Screen Saver"; photo by the author, taken at St. John's College, Oxford University in March 2000.

"Light the Torch of Your Salvation" alludes to critical moments in the biblical story, when God intervened and gave human beings responsibility and power to change the world – Moses at the burning bush (Exodus 3), the Annunciation (Luke 1:26-38), Jesus' baptism (Mark 1:9-11, John 1:32-34), the Spirit descending at Pentecost (Acts 2:1-4), and today (John 6:53-59).

"Black Hole Song" is based on an Associated Press article published in *The Houston Chronicle* September 9, 2003 – "A Song No Human Ear Can Hear: sound from Perseus cluster is 57 octaves below middle C." The poem alludes to the myth of Perseus, son of Zeus, who became invisible when he donned the helmet of Hades.

Publisher Contact Information

Web Site: www.shadowverse.com

Book orders: orders@shadowverse.com

Other requests: info@shadowverse.com

Mailing address: Shadow Verse Press
                        3719 Clover Creek Dr.
                        Kingwood, TX 77345